3x1/06

THE TOMAHAWK CRUISE MISSILE

Matthew Pitt

Children's Press
High Interest Books
A Division of Grolier Publishing
New York / London / Hong Kong / Sydney
Danbury, Connecticut

Contributing Editor: Mark Beyer
Book Design: Michael DeLisio

Photo Credits: Cover, p. 5, 12, 18, 20, 26, 30 © Corbis; p. 6, 9, 15, 16 ©
Photri, Inc.; p. 11 © Reuters/HO-US NAVY/Archive Photos; p. 22 © Reuters/
Bettmann/Corbis; p. 29, 33 © AFP/Corbis; p. 25 © Reuters/Najla Abou
Jahjah/Archive Photos; p. 35 © Bettman/Corbis; p.36 © Yogi, Inc./Corbis; p. 39
© Reuters/Michael W. Pendergrass/Archive Photos; p. 40 © Tim Page/Corbis

Visit Children's Press on the Internet at:
http://publishing.grolier.com

Library of Congress Cataloging-in-Publication Data

Pitt, Matthew.
    The Tomahawk cruise missile / by Matthew Pitt.
    p. cm. – (High-tech military weapons)
    Includes bibliographical references and index.
    Summary: Describes the special features of the Tomahawk missile and
    how this weapon works and provides historical information as well as
    plans for future improvements of the Tomahawk.
    ISBN 0-516-23343-2 (lib. bdg.) – ISBN 0-516-23543-5 (pbk.)
    1. Tomahawk (Guided missile)—Juvenile literature. 2. Cruise missiles—
    Juvenile literature. 3. United States—Armed Forces—Weapons sys-
    tems—Juvenile literature. [1. Tomahawk (Guided missile) 2. Cruise
    missiles.] I. Title. II. Series.

UG1312.C7 P57 2000
623.4'519—dc21

                                                              00-024375

CONTENTS

INTRODUCTION

Flashes of light fill the night air. A rattling sound booms loud as thunder. Smoke and dust clouds appear all around. This is what happens when a Tomahawk cruise missile hits its target. When the United States is forced to go into battle with another nation, it calls on the Tomahawk cruise missile. This missile is dangerous, accurate, and fast. You may have seen these missiles on the evening news. However, reporters don't talk about how a Tomahawk really works. This book does.

Here you will learn what a Tomahawk is and how it works. You will know the missile's history—when it was made, and where it's been used in battle. You'll get to read how the U.S. military plans to make the Tomahawk even better. You also will find out why the U.S. military wants the Tomahawk cruise missiles to help out for years to come!

The Tomahawk missile went through many tests before it was used in combat.

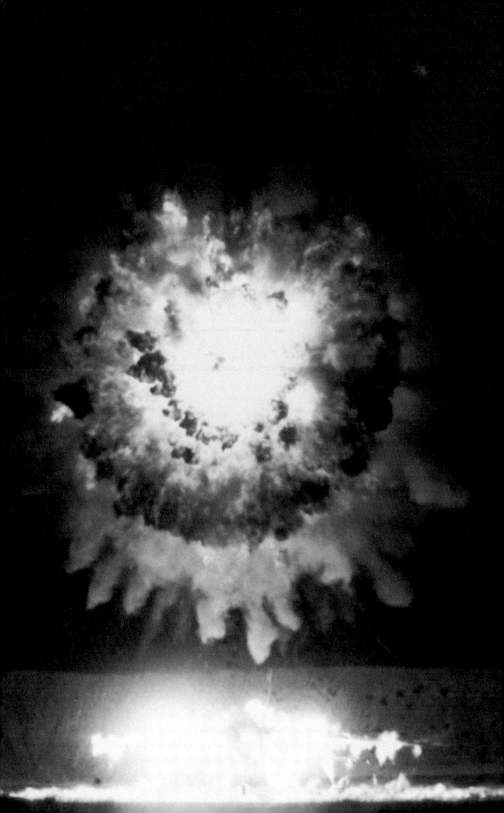

CHAPTER 1

WHAT A TOMAHAWK MISSILE DOES

A Tomahawk is a rocket that has a bomb at the tip of its nose. This type of rocket is called a missile. It's different from rockets that take astronauts into space because it is used for war. The Tomahawk flies long distances at very high speeds. This missile is used to attack targets on the ground. The Tomahawk looks like a winged torpedo, and is about as long as two cars placed end to end. This length is small for a missile. It flies at more than 500 miles per hour. That means it can travel from Detroit, Michigan, to St. Louis,

Tomahawk missiles can be fired from submarines cruising beneath the oceans.

Missouri, in sixty minutes! The Tomahawk can be easily carried, and fired, from many different places. It can be fired from a jet fighter, a ship, or a launch pad on the ground. It even can be fired from a submarine beneath the ocean. Wherever the Tomahawk is fired from, the launch is the same.

READY FOR LIFTOFF!

Tomahawk cruise missiles are launched using computers. Computers are used so that launching errors are avoided. Of course, humans give the computers their orders.

The Tomahawk is fired out of a tube in which it is stored. This tube is called a launcher. Once fired, it takes off toward the sky. A rocket pushes the Tomahawk into the air for the first twelve seconds. This rocket is called a booster. After twelve seconds, the booster uses up its fuel and falls away. At this point, the Tomahawk's wings spread out and

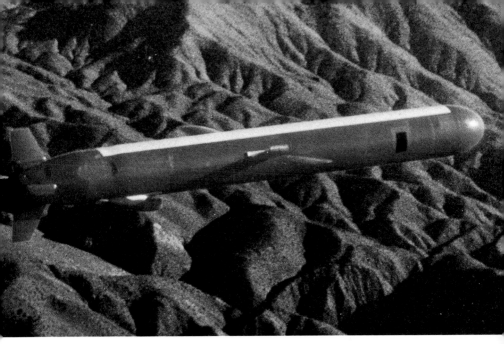

Tomahawk missiles are controlled by computers.

an engine turns on inside the Tomahawk. Now the missile is being flown by an engine, just as an airplane is. This engine is called a turbofan, and it only weighs about 150 pounds. The turbofan engine carries the Tomahawk toward its target. The missile flies the way an airplane does. However, there are many differences between a missile and a plane. One of those differences is that a plane carries its bombs. A Tomahawk is a bomb that flies itself to its target. It flies by computer control.

BOMB OR BOMBLETS?

There are two kinds of Tomahawk missiles. One type is the "C" Tomahawk. This missile carries a single bomb. This bomb holds more than 1,000 pounds of explosives. It is called a warhead. The Tomahawk "C" is used for hitting a single target. The other type of Tomahawk is called the "D." This missile holds a group of smaller warheads. These warheads are called "bomblets." Each bomblet is about the size of a softball. The "D" Tomahawk is used to attack many targets at once. Usually these targets are much smaller than the targets the "C" Tomahawk has to hit, such as trucks or smaller buildings.

THE NUMBER ONE CHOICE

The Tomahawk is used more than any other missile in the U.S. military. There are many reasons for this. The Tomahawk is very good at hitting its targets. This missile is able to fly

Tomahawk missiles launched from battleships keep U.S. military forces safely away from enemy fire.

long distances in a short time. It cannot be seen by the enemy's electronic searching machines, called radar. Dodging the enemy's radar makes the Tomahawk invisible. However, there is one main reason why the U.S. military uses the Tomahawk. The Tomahawk can be launched far away from its target without using a human pilot. This means there is no danger that a U.S. soldier will be killed.

CHAPTER 2

HOW THE TOMAHAWK WORKS

Imagine it's night and you throw a rock as far as you can into a field. A second later you hear a loud sound. It's the sound of the rock hitting metal. Somehow, the rock you tossed hit a soda can in the middle of the field. You'd probably be surprised at hitting that can. You couldn't see the can and you weren't aiming for it. You didn't mean to hit the can. Even if you knew the can was out in the field, it was still dark. You couldn't see the can to aim your throw. You might have to throw a hundred or a thousand rocks to hit that can. Hitting the can the first time was just lucky.

Tomahawk missiles are able to hit targets with pinpoint accuracy.

The Tomahawk cruise missile can do the same thing as the rock that you tossed. The difference is that the success of the Tomahawk is not luck at all. A Tomahawk can hit its intended target over and over again. In fact, people who made the missile say the Tomahawk could be fired in the middle of Utah and hit a target the size of a one-car garage in southern California! If these hits aren't luck, then how can the Tomahawk always hit its target?

1,000 POUNDS--GUIDED BY OUNCES

As are all missiles, Tomahawks are used and launched by trained people. They use computers to aim the missile at a target. After the missile is launched, they also guide the missile to that target. All of this is done using a special computer inside the Tomahawk.

Onboard the missile are tiny computer parts, called circuit boards. They are smaller than your hand. These little computers "talk"

Global positioning satellites (GPS) communicate
with Tomahawk missiles to steer them toward targets.

to a global positioning satellite (GPS). The
GPS satellite flies 12,000 miles above Earth.
The GPS system uses electronic signals to
find a target anywhere on Earth. It also can
tell a missile where to find that target. The
GPS computers help it "see" the ground.
Thanks to this electronic system of com-
puters and satellites, more than 85 percent of
Tomahawk cruise missiles make direct hits
on their targets.

AIRPLANES WITHOUT PILOTS

The GPS helps the Tomahawk find the fastest and safest path to its target. Another computer tells the Tomahawk where to fly. It makes sure the missile doesn't fly into things such as mountains. That computer is called the TER-COM. Its memory has a map of how the ground is shaped. This is called the Earth's terrain. As the Tomahawk flies at its target, the computer reads the map. It makes

sure the missile is flying in the right direction. If the missile goes off course, the computer warns the missile. This warning changes the flight of the missile's path so that it flies in the correct direction again.

This means that the Tomahawks are like airplanes without pilots. The "pilots" are computers controlled by people. Better yet, computer-controlled missiles don't have to worry about clouds or rain. They see through clouds, rain, and other bad weather. They also see at night. This makes their targets defenseless.

HOW GOOD ARE TOMAHAWKS?

Most of the time the Tomahawk cruise missile comes within 30 feet of its target. Even from that far away, the missile will cause a lot of damage. Many Tomahawks have hit right on top of their targets. This is great accuracy when you consider that a Tomahawk's targets are usually hundreds of miles away.

Though unmanned, Tomahawk missiles are controlled by military personnel at control sites on the ground.

CHAPTER 3

THE HISTORY OF THE CRUISE MISSILE

The Tomahawk cruise missile has a long history. It has gone through many changes over the years. Scientists and manufacturers began to develop the missile in 1972. It took them many years to build the missile. In the early 1980s, the Tomahawk "C" and "D" were completed. Both types of missiles carried nuclear bombs. Nuclear bombs are the most destructive kind of bomb ever made.

KEEPING THE PEACE

In the early 1980s, only the United States and the Soviet Union had missiles that could

Tomahawk missiles also can be released from aircraft, such as this B52 Stratofortress.

A 1991 treaty banned cruise missiles
from carrying nuclear weapons.

carry nuclear bombs. Soon, the leaders of both nations understood how dangerous these nuclear bombs were. They knew that if the missiles were ever launched, they would cause terrible destruction of the Earth. A promise was needed not to use these weapons. In 1991, U.S. President George Bush and the leader of the Soviet Union signed a written promise. This written promise is called a treaty. The treaty was a promise to remove all of the nuclear warheads from the cruise missiles. These warheads were later destroyed.

THE MAKING OF A SAFER MISSILE

After the treaty was signed, all Tomahawk cruise missiles were changed. Those carrying nuclear warheads were removed from ships and launching pads. A new type of Tomahawk was made. This new type was cheaper, faster, and more accurate. Also, this new missile used regular explosives (TNT). Now the Tomahawk was safer than the old type of missile. It could not harm the whole Earth when it exploded. In the fall of 1991, the Tomahawk was put to use for the first time in war. It was used against Iraq during the Persian Gulf War.

CHAPTER 4

THE TOMAHAWK'S FIRST TEST

How well would the Tomahawk work in combat? Would it succeed, or would it be an expensive failure? Would it help to end the war? As the Persian Gulf War began in 1991, there were many questions and doubts about the Tomahawk.

MISSION IMPOSSIBLE, OR MISSION ACCOMPLISHED?

When the Persian Gulf War began, the nations allied against Iraq gave their mission a code name. The code name was Operation

One Tomahawk can easily destroy an entire bridge.

Desert Storm. There was one goal of the mission. It was to help free the nation of Kuwait from Iraq's control. Six months earlier, Iraqi soldiers had invaded Kuwait. They wanted the Kuwaiti oil fields and harbors on the Persian Gulf. The United States began to use Tomahawk cruise missiles in combat for the first time. They fired nearly three hundred missiles during Operation Desert Storm. More than 60 percent of those missiles hit their targets. Fifteen of the missiles failed to launch. 20 percent of the missiles either were shot down by the Iraqi military, or failed to hit their targets. Overall, the Tomahawk was thought successful.

Most importantly, the Iraqi military fled Kuwait. The mission was a great success. The Tomahawk missile had performed well in its first mission. However, the makers of the missile didn't celebrate for long. They knew that there was room for improvement. Too

The Tomahawk missile helped win
the Gulf War (1991) against Iraq.

many Tomahawks had failed to hit their targets. Also, some missiles didn't launch correctly. A few booster rocket engines failed to fire when they were supposed to. Military leaders wanted better results from the Tomahawk the next time it was used.

IN ACTION AGAIN

Since the Gulf War, makers of the Tomahawk have tried to make a better missile. They

The explosive power of a Tomahawk
missile packs a tremendous punch.

want the Tomahawk to fly longer distances and be more accurate. They also want to make the missile for less money. Since the Gulf War, the military has given the Tomahawk several chances to prove itself.

The first two chances were against Iraq. The Iraqis had not started another war. However, they were trying to build a nuclear bomb. In January 1993, forty-five Tomahawk cruise missiles were fired at a bomb factory in Iraq. This was just days after Bill Clinton became the new president of the United States. The Iraqi government was trying to make a nuclear weapon of its own. The United States wanted to stop them before they could finish building it. Thirty-seven Tomahawk missiles hit the Iraqi bomb factory.

Later in 1993, the United States fired more missiles toward Iraq. This time, the United States was making the Iraqis pay for a threat they had made. The United States had received reports that the Iraqi government was planning to assassinate former president George Bush. The Tomahawk's target was a military building. Almost every missile hit its target. The plan to assassinate President Bush was stopped.

U.S. military leaders began to notice something. The better the Tomahawk worked, the more chances the U.S. military gave the Tomahawk to succeed. In the past few years, the Tomahawk has been used in Afghanistan, Bosnia, Iraq, and Sudan. Each mission has been different. In Sudan, for example, the missiles were launched at a factory. This factory was believed to be making a deadly chemical weapon. The Tomahawk missiles destroyed the factory. More importantly, the Sudanese people who lived nearby the factory were unharmed. The missiles used in Afghanistan hit targets where terrorists were being trained.

THE KOSOVO MISSION

In 1999, the Tomahawk was used in Kosovo, Yugoslavia. For many years, violence had been spreading in this region. This violence was between two groups of people. On one side were the Serbs. On the other side were the Albanians. The Serbs were led by their president, Slobodan Milosevic. The United States tried peacefully to stop President Milosevic

Tomahawk missiles are able to hit their targets without harming surrounding civilian homes.

and the Serbian army from harming the Albanians. The Serbs didn't want peace. The United States then began a mission called Operation Allied Force. They did this using jet fighters and Tomahawk missiles. The missiles were first used on March 24, 1999. The military operation lasted many weeks. In the end, the Serbs agreed to peace. Many military and political experts believe the Tomahawk helped to end this conflict.

CHAPTER 5

IS THE TOMAHAWK THAT GOOD?

Many people think the Tomahawk cruise missile is a great weapon to have. Military experts around the world know that the missile works. They have seen it used. They know it is powerful and accurate. Plus, the Tomahawk does not need a human to fly it. If the missile is shot down, no one is harmed. Only the enemy will be harmed by its use. So is the Tomahawk a perfect weapon? Not exactly.

Targets hit by Tomahawk missiles are blown apart.

THE TROUBLE WITH THE TOMAHAWK

The people who built the Tomahawk don't think the missile is perfect. The Tomahawk sometimes has problems. It can misfire. It can hit the wrong target. It can hit an obstacle (such as a mountain) before it gets to its target. It also can fail to launch.

Tragic Misses

One of the Tomahawk's worst problems is that sometimes it does miss its targets. This happened many times during the conflict in Kosovo. The missile hit the wrong target. These missiles were aimed at army headquarters, weapons factories, and tanks. Instead, the missiles hit cars, passenger trains, and even homes. These missed targets caused death and destruction to civilians.

One night during an attack, missiles were aimed at what was thought to be a military site. That site turned out to be a health resort

Sometimes a Tomahawk missile misses its target.
This missile hit a civilian apartment complex.

and retirement home. Almost twenty civilians were killed as they slept. Why did this happen? Well, sometimes the computers on the missiles have older maps of targets. They don't know that the target has been moved to a different spot. Computers don't have eyes the way a human pilot does. So when the missiles get close to hitting the ground, the computers think they're aiming at the right target when they really aren't. As accurate as Tomahawks are, they do make mistakes.

Million-Dollar Mistakes

Another problem with the Tomahawk is how much it costs. Each missile costs nearly a million dollars to make. The government doesn't want to buy too many Tomahawk missiles. These missiles are only meant to be used for an emergency. Also, it is expensive when a Tomahawk fails to hit its target. The military cannot use as many missiles as it wants to use. Each one is a big expense. Each missile that fails to work is a million-dollar headache!

WORKING IT OUT WITHOUT WAR

In the end, no country wants to be at war with another. Instead, countries want to solve an argument by talking. Sometimes signing a treaty helps. However, there are times when the military must be used. When a Tomahawk is used by the military, it usually works. It hits its targets without causing

Governments prefer to solve problems with
other countries by signing peace treaties.

fighter pilots or civilians to die needlessly.
The U.S. government hopes that in the years
to come, it won't have any reason to use the
Tomahawk cruise missile.

CHAPTER 6

THE NEED FOR A SMARTER TOMAHAWK

The makers of the Tomahawk are always at the drawing board. They are trying to make the cruise missile faster, cheaper, and more dependable. They do this by testing the missiles. Each year, eight missiles are test-launched (which means the missiles do not hit actual enemy targets). Experts study how these Tomahawks perform. They make sure the missiles work properly. They want to see whether the missiles launch properly. They want to see whether the missiles hit their targets. When missiles don't work properly,

Fire control technicians launch test missiles to study how they act.

these experts find out why. They want to fix any problems before the Tomahawk is used in combat.

TACTICAL TOMAHAWK

As Tomahawk tests continue, there are new types of Tomahawks being built. The first is called the Block IV. It is a tactical Tomahawk. It will do everything the Block III Tomahawk does (the ones being used now). However, it also will do some other things. The Tomahawk Block IV will be able to record how much damage each missile does to its target. This new feature will help the military greatly. If the computer reports that a target is destroyed, another missile won't be wasted on it. The tactical Tomahawk also will be able to take orders. Its mission would be planned just minutes before launch. Plus, military officers will be able to change the missile's orders while it is in the air. This would be the

Air-traffic controllers guide strike
aircraft in and out of enemy territory.

same as your using a remote control to
change the channel on a television. The
Tomahawk can now be told to change its target if that target has moved.

TV GUIDE

Plans are also in place to add TV cameras to
the missiles. Now, officers on the ground can
watch as the Tomahawks fly toward their

targets. If it looks as if a target has been moved to another location, the Tomahawk's flight will be changed. It will be ordered to circle in one spot. The officers would then reprogram the Tomahawk to attack a new target. This new feature will help keep tragedies from happening.

A WAITING GAME

A new type of Tomahawk is expected to be built and ready for use in the year 2003. When it is finished, experts are hoping it will be safer and more accurate than ever. And a future Tomahawk, Block V, will be cheaper. The missile's designers are trying to use easier ways to build Tomahawks at a much lower cost. You can see how much work people have done to make the Tomahawk succeed. Its record of success is getting better. The Tomahawk will be the United States' weapon of choice in times of war for years to come.

Smart missiles are equipped with cameras to help them hit their targets. This technology will be used on the new Tomahawk missile ready for use in 2003.

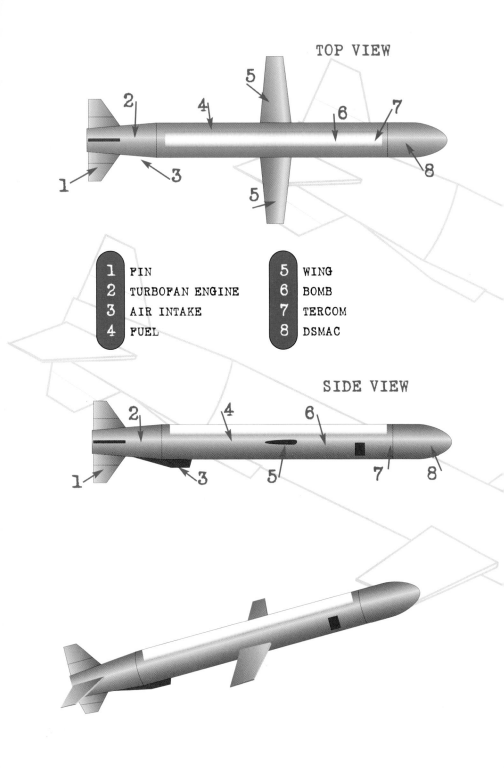

TOP VIEW

SIDE VIEW

1	FIN	5	WING
2	TURBOFAN ENGINE	6	BOMB
3	AIR INTAKE	7	TERCOM
4	FUEL	8	DSMAC

long-range subsonic cruise
missile for striking high
value or heavily defended
land targets.

WARHEAD:	1,000 lb. - W80 250 Kiloton Thermonuclear or 1,000 lb. Conventional High Explosive/Fragmentary
RANGE:	1,553 miles
WINGSPAN:	8 feet 9 inches
LENGTH:	18 feet 3 inches; with booster: 20 feet 6 inches
WEIGHT:	4,190 pounds
ENGINE:	Solid Propellent Booster/Turbojet Cruise one Williams F107-400 rated at 600 lbs. thrust
GUIDANCE:	TERCOM, GPS, DSMAC and INFRA-RED
SPEED:	550 miles per hour
COST:	$4 million to $2 million, depending on version

NEW WORDS

assassinate to murder a famous or important person

booster a rocket that increases an engine's power and speed

bomblets a group of small bombs

civilians people who are not in military service

reliable something that can be trusted

treaty a written promise, often between two or more nations

turbofan the small engine inside a Tomahawk cruise missile

warhead a bomb

FOR FURTHER READING

Byam, Michelle. *Arms and Armor.* New York: Alfred A. Knopf Books for Young Readers, 1988.

Italia, Bob. *Weapons of War.* Minneapolis: ABDO Publishing Company, 1991.

Macknight, Nigel. *Tomahawk Cruise Missile.* Osceola, WI: MBI Publishing Company, 1995.

Nichols, John R. *Air Defense Weapons.* Vero Beach, FL: Rourke Enterprises, 1989.

RESOURCES

The Air Force Armament Museum
100 Museum Drive
Eglin Air Force Base, FL 32542
(904) 882-4062
Web site: *www.wg53.eglin.af.mil/armmus/
default.htm*

Web Sites
The United States Navy-Navy Fact File
*www.chinfo.navy.mil/navpalib/factfile/
missiles/wep-toma.html*
This site gives detailed facts about the
Tomahawk cruise missile. Learn about its
special features and background.

How Cruise Missiles Work
www.howstuffworks.com/cruise.htm
Learn more about how cruise missiles work.
This site also contains links to other related
sites.

INDEX

INDEX

About the Author

Matthew Pitt is a freelance writer living in Brooklyn, New York. He has written several magazine articles and short stories while living in cities such as Austin, Texas; Washington D.C.; and Los Angeles, California.